I0145031

LAWS OF PROSPERITY

A Spiritual Guide to Earthly Successes

Rev. Dr. Della Reese Lett

Lett/Reese International Publishing Company

All Rights Reserved.

This book may not be reproduced in whole or in part in any way without permission.

Copyright © 2010

Lett/Reese International Publishing Company

PO Box 24567

Los Angeles, CA 90024

ISBN: 978-0-578-04590-0

Production Manager: Wally White

Production Coordinator: Jodi Smith

Cover Photograph: Cliff Lipson

Cover Design: Franklin Lett

Cover Graphic Design and Layout: Sean Stearley

Laws of Prosperity

PREFACE

My mother was and really still is my hero although she left this planet in 1949. She was my hero and the wind beneath my wings. She gave me what was necessary to rise up and out of the slums of Detroit, Michigan.

Because of her beliefs, attitudes and understanding of God, she had a personal relationship with God. I have had a relationship with God all my life; my mother required it. She used her relationship to feed us sometimes, heal us sometimes and although there were few luxuries, there was great love and peace of mind.

Leaving home for my chosen career when I was seventeen, after my mother died all I had was my talent and the understandings my mother had taught me, engrained in me is more like it. They are responsible for my being able to work in the world and not be of it.

One day thirty-two years ago I walked into a church in Chicago, Illinois and heard a woman expressing the thoughts my mother had taught me. She was using different words but the meanings were the same. Positive faith and the witnessing to the actual use of prayer and faith for living in a better way here and now!

I had to know her, and I am proud to say I have that privilege. Reverend Dr. Johnnie Colemon is "My Buddy" and through her teaching I gained a metaphysical understanding. She taught me how to see my REAL SELF, the one Jesus Christ came to teach us about, the self that is made in the image likeness of God.

The self, filled with the power of God placed inside of me, so that I (we) may have life and that more abundantly, through understanding, prayer, meditation and faith.

Dr. Colemon of course introduced me to many branches of knowledge. I have had the privilege to study the works of Reverend Dr. Colemon, Charles Fillmore, George Lamsa, H. Emilie Cady, Catherine Ponder, Rocco Errico, Joseph Murphy, Robert A. Russell, Elizabeth Sand Turner, Jack Ensign Addington, Georgiana Tree West and Joel S. Goldsmith to name a few.

Since God is the Truth, has always been the Truth, and God never changes, this is by no means a new TRUTH. For there is no new Truth, and no DIFFERENT TRUTH, only God and more God unchanging. There are many things in this book you have heard or seen or even thought about on your own. This is just the way I have taught these lessons and seen the benefits to the lives of my congregation, and I would like to share them. I believe with Jesus, "Whosoever will, let him come."

Let him come, and "study, show thyself approved unto God, a workman that needs not to be ashamed rightly dividing the word of truth." 2Timothy 2:15

The lessons in this book are transcribed from live sermons I have given at Understanding Principles for Better Living Church in Los Angeles, CA. I have a way of pausing to give my listeners a moment to think or question themselves. I stop, say "Huh," and then continue. When you see that throughout this book, I invite you to take those same moments to think and question yourself.

Rev. Della

PROSPERITY IS GOD'S IDEA

Prosperity is a (my) state of mind, and (my) feelings.

Prosperity is the ability to do what you (I) want; to do when you (I) want to do it.

True prosperity includes an abundance of all the good things in life. Good health, right relationships, satisfying work and a more than ample supply of money.

Jesus talked more about money or supply than any other subject, so He must have realized its importance. I realize its importance.

Moses told the Hebrew people, "You shall remember the Lord your God, for it is He who gives you power to get wealth." Deuteronomy 8:18

"I am the Lord thy God which teaches you to profit, which leads you by the way you should go."

Isaiah 48:17

"They shall prosper that love Thee. " Psalm 122:6

I love the Lord with all of my heart, soul, mind, body, being and strength. I cannot help but prosper.

PROSPERITY IS GOD'S IDEA

"Eye hath not seen nor ear heard, neither have entered into the heart of man the things which God hath prepared for them that love Him."

1 Corinthians 2:9

"They that seek the Lord shall not want any good thing."

Psalm 34:10

I embrace the idea of my God that I should be prosperous.

I see myself as the prosperous child of a loving Father.

I am God's idea. I am prosperity and that more abundantly.

I mean, He decided that before this group of people ever got on the planet Earth; long, long before our group came!

Eons ago, He decided we should have the very best of everything. So, it's time for you to start expecting and accepting in the name of God.

WORKING INSIDE THE LAW

I tell you this all the time, "If God is your partner, make your plans larger."

I'll tell you again, "If God is your partner, make your plans larger."

You need the confidence to step out of your comfort zone of small things, and small thinking, to be able to let your mind work instead of your back.

You need to trust what your mind tells you. Because the Christ in you controls the kind of life we all really want. The one filled with peace and prosperity and that more abundantly.

And it expresses through you, to you; leading you to your highest good, no matter the appearances.

You need to work with your imagination to do that. You need to be able to see, by your faith, that your dreams are already realities.

You need to be able to conceive wonderful things and marvelous situations and relationships. You need to see it so clearly, that your faith becomes a reality!

And you know for sure, that you know what you know.

And that what you have conceived and now believe, you shall receive. You need peace to do that; to make your plans larger, I mean.

Why? Because you cannot be creative and at the same time be worried, anxious, doubtful and disturbed; and make larger plans.

You need the awareness that nothing can disturb the calm peace of your soul.

You need to give up any and all versions and concepts of lack or limitations.

You need to be able to allow your wealth to circulate. Not only your money.

Your wealth of ideas
Your thoughts
Your warmth as a human being
Your understanding
Your assistance
Your love
Your money and appreciation
You and the fullness thereof

You need love to do that. You need unconditional God love to do that. You need a love that you do not charge people for.

You need a love that you do not bind people with, because you cannot afford to be bound. What you bind to you; to that you are bound.

You need a love that flows freely that you do not have to work for; the reason being, you don't have time for that.

You need to make decisions. You need to decide what goes into the file cabinet and what goes into the trash bin.

If God is your partner, you need to learn to think larger thoughts. You need to broaden your mind and your desires and dreams.

That's a lot...wow...that's a lot!

God knew that it was a lot! So, He gave us the laws that will work for us, if we work inside of The Law.

The purpose of this lesson is to show you that you can use The Law to lift yourself out of the place where you are. To the place where you rightfully belong because, if God is your partner, you can make your plans larger.

Your right place is where you can enjoy success and plenty, naturally, as the Father intended. We will study The Law so you can make your plans larger.

We will start with "The Law of Compensation." Well, look a here, we're back at the same place again, "Whatever a man soweth, that shall he also reap."

Inevitably, our own comes to us and only what is our own. Compensation means equal return for that which is given. It means a balance of that quality or service that is extended to another.

The Law inevitably produces its own exactness as a rule of action. We are free agents to choose the method of procedure in our lives.

The Law helps those who help themselves. The Law of Compensation always works that way.

Whatever you're getting from your life is yours! You made the investment and what you are getting is your return on your investment. It belongs to you only!

The Law of Compensation is both a good and effective law. The Law does not need to change. Neither success nor prosperity needs to be made, they already are.

If you are not the proud owner of:

- † Success, prosperity and confidence
- † A working imagination
- † Peace of mind
- † Love
- † Big thoughts making big dreams come true

...somewhere you have miscalculated. You've made a mistake. You've sinned; if you will.

WORKING INSIDE THE LAW

"Be not conformed to this world. But be ye transformed by the renewing of your mind, that ye may prove what is that good, and acceptable, and perfect will of God."

Romans 12:2

If you add 2 + 2 and you keep getting 9, you have miscalculated because there is nothing wrong with the science of mathematics.

You cannot use The Law to suit your mistakes.

You must change your use of The Law to its correct application. Successful living is a science, and there are laws governing this science. The supply and the possibility is ever the same and always at hand.

It is our part to change our use or application of The Law to correctness, in order to bring about better conditions in our lives, worlds and affairs.

Once you change your mind, you see things differently and you will therefore do things differently and you will then be able to change your conditions.

It is only when you stop recognizing a condition that you stop attracting it to you. What you have your mind on has its mind on you.

The principle involved is that when you, hear me good now, when you become too large for your present place, you will begin to draw yourself to something larger.

You cannot attract the bigger or the better until you first become larger.

Have you ever heard the expression, "Water seeks its own level"? If you grow larger spiritually and mentally, the Law of Compensation will advance you to a larger place. The Law of Compensation is why we have progress, growth, development and evolution.

Jesus included The Law of Compensation as a supreme factor in His doctorate:

"Give and it shall be given to you."

"Judge not that ye be not judged."

"With all measure that you mete, it shall be measured unto you."

"Do unto others as you would them do unto you."

"Whatever a man soweth, so shall he also reap."

"All things work together for the good of those who love the Lord."

Think of whatever experience you are challenged with right now and say this aloud:

"In the depth of my being I know that my Father loves me.

I know that in His absolute good way, He wants only the best for me.

I accept that, in all situations and circumstances and I praise Him in an attitude of gratitude!"

There are a few points common in everyday life where we tend to fall into a snare:

† Don't expect something for nothing. Pay your own way.

† Don't stand back and let the other person pay. For if he pays, The Law of Compensation must work for him, because he/she is always sowing. So, he must always reap.

† Don't hunt for cheap. If you find a bargain, well and good, but don't make your level of buying a bargain level in purchases, thoughts and/or actions.

† Do not begrudge spending money. Stop hating to pay your bills. Release your money cheerfully, even *if* it does seem to be the last dollar you can see that you have at this moment. Holding back closes the channel, the faucet which is limiting supply from pouring in, on and over you.

The owner of a prosperity consciousness cannot be impoverished. With this understanding, let us invite our Father and our Wayshower, Jesus Christ, into our use of divine law.

"My Invitation to My Father"

Father, I invite You and allow You to create through me. Give me the mental attitude to stretch out on Your word; obeying Your laws and accomplishing my desires and dreams.

I replace inferior thoughts with superior thoughts; evil thoughts with good thoughts; distressing thoughts with pleasant thoughts. I mentally and consciously look for the God in me, which is the good in me.

My spiritual supply is always available. It never runs out, and it will yield according to my faith demands upon it.

The "Law of Compensation" is my law. God gave it to me to govern my good. I use it so my life will be a better place to live in.

THE LAW OF THINKING

We have been working with The Law in order to attain a sense of oneness with life and to get a greater understanding of the same spiritual laws that enabled Jesus to do the great works He did.

Jesus taught, "All things are possible to them that believe." "Whatsoever you pray and ask for, believing that you have received them, and you shall have them."

The state of your mind determines your progress. It also determines the state of your affairs.

Every object, circumstance and form in this world, including the world, is purely mental. God created the world and everything out of His creative mind.

If the ruling state of your mind is broad, optimistic and true to spiritual law, your mental state will correspond to true spiritual law. You will show constructive progressions toward your manifesting.

We attract only what we think or create and accept as true.

So, what do we do about this? We rise above any limitation by organizing our thinking along constructive lines that produce what we want.

THE LAW OF THINKING

Hear me clearly now...

Your thought is the connecting link between God and you.

Secondly, you are not what you think you are, you are what you think.

Really hear me good now!

Since we are made in the image likeness of God, we have the great ability to think. It's our power to think, and how we use our power to think that determines our state of living.

Our thoughts affect our welfare and often affect others we think of.

Thoughts are things and things are thoughts.

"Commit thy works unto the Lord and thy thoughts shall be established."   Proverbs 16:3

Pray, speaking the words of truth, claiming your good, thinking about it with expectation. Know this; your thinking about it constructively produces it.

Did you get that? The Law of Mind (thinking) is in perpetual operation and it works both ways. If your mind dwells on thoughts of failure and poverty, you will move yourself into those conditions.

THE LAW OF THINKING

What you have your mind on, has its mind on you. What you hold in your mind, takes form in your outer world.

"As a man thinketh in his heart so is he."

Proverbs 23:7

You cannot stop thinking. You are constantly thinking. Thoughts are constantly flitting across your mind. The glorious thing is that you can change your thoughts.

"Judge the righteous judgment" John 7:24

Q: What is the righteous judgment?

A: Right thinking followed by right action.

> **"All things work together for the good of those who love the Lord!"**
>
> **I love the Lord!**
>
> **"It is my Father's good pleasure to give me the kingdom of heaven."**
>
> **"I can do all things through Christ who strengthens me."**

Thinking is the movement of thoughts and ideas in the mind.

THE LAW OF THINKING

Thinking is the process by which we arrive at conclusions and from those conclusions we form:

- † Mental Images
- † Pictures
- † Beliefs, based on our understanding of our ideas

By this process we bring our ideas into manifestation in our lives in exact proportion of the interpretation of the idea held in our mind.

Right thinking is a form of praying and a form of praising. For example, I think Matthew 21:22 is the truth, and so for me it *is* the truth.

> **"All things whatsoever I shall ask in prayer believing, I shall receive!"**

I think that Luke 11:9-10 is the truth and so for me it is the truth. I believe it, so I can bring it forth in my life in whatever instance or form I need it to be in.

"Ask, and it shall be given you; seek and ye shall find; knock and it shall be opened unto you. For everyone that asks receives; and he that seeks finds; and to him that knocks it shall be opened."

Luke 11:9-10

THE LAW OF THINKING

Jesus, who I have claimed as my Wayshower for all things (Did you get that? ALL THINGS – that's anything that is for my highest good), told Matthew and Luke to tell me these things. I believe these things, so they are operative truth for me.

Think about that. I mean really think about that.

When you think something is the truth, you believe it. And since I believe Jesus' promises when I pray, I just have to ask for it, in His name; seek it out; knock on the entry ways to have them open for me. Goodbye worry. Goodbye fear. Goodbye need. Goodbye all negativity.

Because the state of my mind determines my progress and I am now thinking righteously, I know my proper place and I stay in it.

"If you abide in me and my words abide in you [Della], *you shall ask what you will and it shall be done unto you."*
John 15:7

The prophet Jeremiah brings me word from my Father God:

"Call unto Me and I will answer thee, and show thee great and mighty things which thou knowest not."
Jeremiah 33:3

Goodbye doubt. No wondering what to do because of my right thinking followed by right action.

I think as long as I call my Father, He will answer when I call unto Him. I think He knows everything, so I have but to stand on my faith, anticipating great and mighty things, which I do not know yet.

Fear get out of my face because I think I have help in trouble, and fear is a whole lot of trouble.

"For I am persuaded, (I think, I believe) *that neither death, nor life, nor angels, nor principalities, nor powers, nor things present, nor things to come, nor height, nor depth, nor any other creature shall be able to separate me, from the love of God, which is in Christ Jesus our Lord."*

Romans 8:38-39

We must stop using what Paul referred to as "the mind of the flesh" (believing what the carnal mind says); it is death, it brings sorrow, trouble, and sickness.

But the mind of the Spirit has the ability to still the carnal mind and let the Spirit speak within us and that is life and peace.

THE LAW OF THINKING

"Eye hath not seen nor ear heard, neither have entered into the heart of man, the things which God hath (not will have, it's already done for you) *prepared for them that love Him."*

1 Corinthians 2:9

"Be ye transformed by the renewing of your mind."

Romans 12:2

Change your mind and change your life. Change your thinking and you will change your beliefs. Change your beliefs to the positiveness of God, which will change your conditions to the higher standards God intended for you.

You have to already know for sure that the *"foolishness of God is wiser than men."*

1 Corinthians 1:25

The time has seriously come for us *"...to have the mind in us which was also in Christ Jesus."*

Philippians 2:5

Your intellect is the servant to the real mind, your spiritual mind. Our way of thinking makes our happiness or unhappiness, our success or nonsuccess. We can, by effort, change our ways of thinking. No matter how the appearances present themselves to us we must always continue to think.

God is at all times, regardless of our situation and or circumstances. He is trying to pour more good into our lives to make them richer and more successful.

But remember, the state of our mind determines our progress and the state of our affairs.

God can only do for you what He can do through you and your thoughts; your thinking about it constructively produces it.

Think that...until you can believe that, and then take the righteous road. Thinking is our intellect in action, which allows us to reason, choose, comprehend; and gives us the will to act.

There is no limit to the scope of your mind, because there is only one mind and that is God's mind.

We are just plugged into it and we can plug into whatever we need or whatever we need to know.

Q: Have you ever noticed that some people command the utmost respect and that those who do, are the most successful people?

Q: Have you noticed that some people receive the "Hey girl" and the "Hey man" while there are others who receive the "Yes, Ma'am" and the "Yes, Sir" treatment?

THE LAW OF THINKING

Q: Have you noticed that the "Yes Sir," "Yes Ma'am" group are commanding and confident almost to royalty? (Extracting admiration, while other people do not.)

Ever wonder about that? Why is that so? What is the explanation for that?

It is the "Yes Ma'am," "Yes Sir" thinking! Thinking does make it so. Others see in us what we see in ourselves. We receive the kind of treatment we think we deserve.

If you think you are inferior, regardless of what your real qualifications are, you are inferior. Thinking regulates actions; so if you feel inferior you will act that way! No veneer or cover-up or fluff will hide for long that you feel inferior, if you feel you are not important, you are right; you are not important.

You are in charge of your life, for God has given you power, dominion and mastery and His authority to use them. Therefore, whatever you say is so in your life — it is so in your life. If you think, feel, say, act, and react as if you are important, you will be. How you think determines how others react to you. To command respect you must first think you deserve respect.

The more respect you have for yourself, the more respect others will have for you.

Self-respect shows through in everything we do. Your mind is the gateway to wisdom, knowledge, understanding and power. If you want to experience anything, you must first think it deeply enough to know it in your mind.

Anything. Anything, do you hear me? Anything. Anything that is known and accepted in your mind, consciously and subconsciously, must become a fact in your experience.

It is The Law of Cause and Effect. The cause is always in the mind; in the form of:

† Urges

† Desires

† Attitudes

† Opinion

† Convictions

† Feelings

† Thoughts and Ideas

These are all mental activities. Your mind is your consciousness. It is a superb tool with which you mold objects and experiences out of the raw stuff.

We have the unformed intelligence, the substance which is God. Stop being afraid of your mind and make it your friend. Recognize what you think. Train your mind to think constructive and creative thoughts.

Discipline your mind not to think things that are destructive to you. Praise it for the magnificent thing that it is. Use it more definitely. Don't just let it roam around uselessly.

Get definite with your thoughts; get specific and logical. Don't take every little thing so seriously, especially yourself. You become great through perseverance. You just have to keep at it. Be thorough whatever you do... do it well.

Learning detachment is necessary! Don't become personally responsible for every crook in the road. Do your part and the results will take care of themselves. Get it clear in your mind what you really want. Form a clear picture and take it step by step. Don't be so uptight, put some humor in it.

Edgar Guest said, "The man worthwhile is the man who can smile when everything is going dead wrong." You can do that when your mind knows, no matter how dead it looks, it is an appearance and I will not judge by appearances. I will judge the righteous judgment and I know…

"All things, even this, is working for the good of those who love the Lord and I love the Lord."

THE LAW OF THINKING

The preacher said in Proverbs, *"A merry heart doeth good like a medicine, a broken spirit drieth the bones."*

Proverb17:22

Do you think about your spirituality? If you do think about your spirituality, what do you think of your spirituality? How do you use your connecting link between you and God? Do you control your mind or do you just let it run wild with nothingness and waste?

Are you plugged in tightly or are you hanging on by a thread?

Are you unfolding or are you stagnant?

Do you ever think about God? If so, what do you think? What is your attitude about God? What do you think God thinks about you?

What are your desires about God, from God, with God? How do you want God to be in your life, world, and affairs? What are you urged to do with God?

When you need to commune with Him, do you persevere or are you in a hurry? Do you have fun with God? Do you go to Him in a light state of mind and share the good things He has done for you or just when there is pain?

Bill Pittman has a line in a song he wrote, "You can't even call His name unless you are in pain."

Is that all you think God is good for? Do you show your love for Him by your obedience to His word? Do you do what He says because you love Him or for the reward?

"As a man thinketh in his heart so is he," and that goes for women too. Think about it!

The glorious thing is that you can change your thoughts about any condition and "judge the righteous judgment."

What is the righteous judgment in this case? *"All things work together for the good of those who love the Lord." "It is the Father's good pleasure to give me the kingdom of heaven." "I can do all things through Christ who strengthens me."* We attract only what we think or create and accept as true.

So, what do we do about this? We rise above any limitation by organizing our thinking along constructive lines; your thoughts between you and God. You are who you think you are.

Really hear me good now!

Every object, circumstance and form in this world is purely mental. If the ruling state of your mind is broad, optimistic and true to spiritual law, your mental state will correspond with and show, constructive progressiveness.

THE LAW OF ADJUSTMENT

The Divine Law of Adjustment
The Ability for Adaptability

God will not adjust Himself to our ways. We cannot expect God to adjust Himself to our ways because God is not stupid! It is up to us to make the adjustment through our adaptability to His ways, with His ways, for His way; is the only way.

It is a waste of time to ask "Why?" when problems arise. Implicit in every problem is the right answer, as to the right way to go. It is up to us to make use of our built-in capacity to bring out the best of life in each day's living. Each day's living is different.

Life seems to be an endless series of challenges and difficulties. There is, however in life, that system that works incessantly to resolve conflicts, to heal ills and to establish peace and fulfillment.

This system is the Divine Law of Adjustment; the ability to adapt. Jesus said, *"I came that they may have life and may have it abundantly."* He was talking about a discovery that forms the central idea of His gospel or "good news".

The great idea is simply this: Because we are spiritual beings, we are forever the focus of a spiritual power that works to manifest life, in perfect health and harmony and abundance.

We cannot get away from this spiritual power even if we don't use it; it is still there waiting for us to use it.

Jesus identified this power as "the Father within us." Jesus said, *"...it is the Father within me that does the work"*

John 14:10

"It is our Father's good pleasure to give us the keys to the kingdom."

Luke 12:32

"The Father knows the things you have need of before you ask Him."

Matthew 6:8

"All things whatsoever the Father has are mine."

John 16:15

We never know how He will supply our needs, and we don't have to because that's God's business. We just need to know that He will. Since we don't know how He will do it, we must be able to adjust or adapt to the will of God and to His plan for our lives.

Divine Law is the intelligence of God that is working always, constantly, instantly and abundantly.

THE LAW OF ADJUSTMENT

You must not be stuck in the mud with only one solution. God is many, many, (and add a zillion more many's), faceted.

We must adapt. We must adjust to God's intelligence. When we desire our good, we make plans and we have in mind how it should be wrapped, what color the box should be and when it should arrive.

It is true we must be specific with the universe, but you cannot dictate to God, who sees the panoramic view, while we only see through a hole in the fence, down a tunnel that is dark along the way, showing only a light in the great distance.

Because of His vantage viewpoint, how, who brings it, however it gets here, what color and kind of a box it is in — are all decisions for the Father.

You may already have what you need and you just need to adjust or adapt yourself to its change of form.

Now there cried a certain woman of the wives of the sons of the prophets unto Elisha saying, "thy servant my husband is dead, and thou knowest that thy servant did fear the Lord; and the creditor is come to take unto Him my two Sons to be bondmen.

And Elisha said unto her, "What shall I do for thee? Tell me what hast thou in the house?"

THE LAW OF ADJUSTMENT

And she said, "Thine handmaid hath not anything in the house, save a pot of oil."

Then he said, "Go borrow thee vessels abroad of all thy neighbours, even empty vessels; borrow not a few. And when thou art come in though shalt shut the door upon thee and upon all thy sons, and shalt pour out into all those vessels, and thou shalt set aside that which is full."

And so she went from him, and shut the door upon her and upon her sons, who brought the vessels to her; and she poured out.

And it came to pass, when the vessels were full, that she said unto her son, "Bring me yet a vessel." And he said unto her, "There is not a vessel more." And the oil stayed.

Then she came and told the man of God. And he said, "Go sell the oil and pay thy debt, and live thou and thy children of the rest." 2 Kings 4:1-7

Do not stop until you have filled the situation or circumstance or condition up to the brim. It wouldn't hurt to run it over the brim.

You have to adjust and sometimes readjust. You must persist in the use of your ability for adaptability. Until you fill the situation "to the brim," knowing when you persist, your good cannot resist.

THE LAW OF ADJUSTMENT

This is not the time for "We always did it this way or that way for as long as I can remember" or "I ain't never heard of doing it that way before."

Get up to this please! God does not need anyone or anything to set precedence for Him. He can do it any way He wants to, when He wants to, for as little or as long as He wants to.

We have to be flexible, adaptable, able to adjust to His plans. It is a degree by degree process. The old hymn says, "you can't hurry God, you have to wait my brother, just obey His word that you have heard." And that's the truth!

The longer God is in coming, the greater it will be when it comes. So hold onto God's unchanging hand. What do you care how He blesses you... just so He blesses you.

Why can't you wait when He has given you His word that The Law will work if you work it? If we don't like the person bringing the blessing, or we don't like the way it's wrapped (so to speak), or because that's not the way we planned it — we turn away our good.

God always has a better plan than ours because He has a better view of all of life. He knows the right time and the right place for your good to come to you in a perfect way, when you are ready to handle it.

THE LAW OF ADJUSTMENT

You cannot come up short dealing with God. You cannot fail following His word. The way your good is delivered may seem strange and sometimes you are unable to see that this way will bring you new and exciting situations and opportunities that will propel you and your life, world, and affairs into a gratifying adventure you've never known before.

When you take stock of your inner abilities, your outer supply may be inclined to say, "there is not enough to go around." That's when you must remember there may not be enough of <u>your</u> abilities, but there is enough God to go around and around and around again and again and again and infinitum.

"All the Father is, I am. And all the Father has, is mine."

THE LAW OF ADJUSTMENT

Say this aloud:

"There is more than enough to go around and around as many times as necessary, I am capable of adapting my mind to this truth.

I now follow through on God's definite word and specific plans that I act upon with faith. I have adjusted my computer (my mind), and I have adapted this philosophy.

When I persist, my good cannot resist. When I persist, my good cannot resist. I am a God-made magnet and I attract my good and nothing but my good always in the name of Christ Jesus. When I persist, my good cannot resist because I can adjust and adapt, as needed."

THE LAW OF CHANGE

"Everything must change, nothing ever stays the same. Everyone must change. Nothing and no one goes unchanged. The young become old and mysteries do unfold. That's the way of time. Nothing goes unchanged." ~ Bernard Ighner

You might ask or wonder why. Our contract says in Ecclesiastes 3:1 -8,

"To everything there is a season and a time to every purpose under the heaven: a time to be born and a time to die; a time to plant and a time to pluck up that which is planted.

A time to kill and a time to heal, a time to break down and a time to build up; a time to weep and a time to laugh; a time to case away stones and a time to gather stones together; a time to embrace and a time to refrain from embracing; a time to get and a time to lose; a time to keep and a time to cast away; a time to rend and a time to sew; a time to keep silence and a time to speak; a time of war and a time of peace. "

...because there is a season and a time to every purpose. Everything must and will be changing at all times. Change is a success-power. Did you know that? We shouldn't resist or resent change.

THE LAW OF CHANGE

It is the natural order of things. Change is necessary because it is a time of growth and it is good. Our human nature is inclined to resist change, but the spiritual nature insists upon change. A change indicates that *"your growing is showing"*.

Hear me good now. It's not the changes that hurt you, it is your resistance to the changes that you beat yourself with. Resisting change stops your growth. You have to learn to welcome change. When you do, you are welcoming another chance to grow.

Emmett Fox once said, *"I see the angel of God in every change."* Your soul demands change for its growth. The creating of new good takes place in the midst of change. The death of the old is the birth of the new.

You fail when you hold onto the past; that would be bad enough. But after all is said and done, whatever it is, when it is time for it to go, you will have to let go; before or after the fight.

Change will still come but through unpleasant experiences; you will literally be shocked into letting go. When change comes through bitter experiences, it tries your faith. Unless you have an active faith, you get confused and frustrated. There are tell-tale signs when a change is coming.

THE LAW OF CHANGE

Those of you, who have a constant communion with God, know that the Holy Spirit never lets anything slip up on you. You know, even though sometimes you don't know why until after the fact. You get restless and dissatisfied when you get near the end of a cycle in your growth process.

You get that way with a situation that has up to now, been satisfactory. You are no longer satisfied to go on living as you have in the past. So, you don't work at it as you used to and you begin to fall into it.

Nothing goes right anymore.

Eventually, you begin to fail where you were previously successful in it, or with it, or as it. Whatever it is, becomes unfriendly, often hostile, definitely inharmonious to you and no matter what you do, you cannot fix it!

It no longer cooperates with you because it is releasing you to your new good elsewhere. You may as well be through with it and release it because it is through with you and it will eat you up until you do release it and change.

Failure is success trying to be born in a bigger way in your life. Old ways must die. Failure is only the death of those old ways so that the new one hundred-fold increase of blessings may follow.

THE LAW OF CHANGE

If one particular talent is no longer needed, it may be because you have become so satisfied with that one ability that you have ceased to expand and grow in other ways. You just live in your comfort zone.

You may not have been aware of it, but your soul has been reaching out toward greater possibilities.

It's time for a change.

Don't get bound by or to old ideas, relationships or environments. Let things fall away as they will, as you begin to grow. If you don't hold them too tightly to you, they will fall away thus you make the change.

Don't allow ("let not") yourself to become so fixed to certain ways of living that you cannot be happy if or when those things change. God is the only permanent initiate.

Everything must change and some changes are beautiful and some are not. Good, bad or indifferent, there will be changes. And if each one that occurs knocks you down you're going to be awfully sore all over.

What difference should the changes make to you whatever they are? Unless you don't know that, *"All things work together for the good of those who love the Lord,"* even more so in changes, you cannot bypass change. You can temporarily avoid it which is a real horror. Because while you are trying to avoid it, the change is taking place and you are at the wrong place at the wrong time. So you don't ride the crest of the wave, which is the spiritual way, you get swept down in the undertow.

You may not even be in the same set of circumstances when you are forced to change. You place yourself in the place where you have to be, at the mercy of reaction instead of using your power of action.

Change is the master Law of Life since it is The Law of Nature to grow. To really live is to grow and to grow is to change. Sometimes, the loss seems unbearable. Sometimes, just that kind of a loss is what you need to work the necessary revolutions out in your life.

That kind of loss forces you to terminate what was and allow the formation of a new, more adequate, more friendly change to your new you.

If you look back in your life, you will see that some drastic change proves to be the basis for what happened that was important to the next few years of your life. Hold fast in the time of change and fail, let go and let God and you will grow in success.

When it seems you have lost hold of the situation, it is because you are supposed to lose your hold on it. You're supposed to let it go so that the new good may appear. Don't keep trying to hold onto it or get it back. Let it go!

There is something much better in store for you. You cannot play with the same toys all of your life. Get some new toys.

Don't you remember how much fun it was to get new toys? We can reap the vast benefits of the acceleration of change when we recognize change for what it is:

"Expansion into greater good."

Say this aloud:

"Without fear of change, with the understanding of change, I am expanding into my greater good!"

THE LAW OF GIVING AND RECEIVING

I am a miracle in the making through the "The Law of Giving & Receiving."

My church is named "Understanding Principles for Better Living" on purpose!

"Give me understanding and I shall keep thy law, yea I shall observe it with my whole heart." Psalm 119:34

"Get wisdom! Get understanding; forget it not; neither decline from the words of my mouth. Forsake her (wisdom) not, and she shall preserve thee.

Wisdom is the principle thing; therefore, get wisdom: and with all thy getting, get understanding.

*Exalt her (*understanding*) and she shall promote thee; she shall bring thee to honor, when thou dost embrace her.*

*She (*understanding*) shall give to thine head an ornament of grace; a crown of glory shall she deliver to thee."*

Proverbs 4:5-9

Understanding reduces the greatest wonderment to simplicity. The lack of understanding causes the least things to take on the magnitude of complexity. In order to make Christianity practical, we have got to understand Christianity and obey the laws upon which it is founded.

THE LAW OF GIVING AND RECEIVING

God exists in us as His highest concept of perfection and comes forth through us; through our faith as love, intelligence and power.

In a state of limited understanding, you reason that you must get before you can give. When The Law is:

"Give and it shall be given unto you; good measure, pressed down, shaken together and running over will be put into your bosom. For with the same measure you use it shall be measure back to you." Luke 6:38

The plain fact is that it is The Law of Life that as we think, speak and act towards others, so will others think, speak and act toward us. This is a definite place for a correct understanding because it will save you a lot of unfulfilled and hurt feelings.

Because this in no way means that the same people we treat wonderfully will be the person to return our action. In fact, that is very, very rarely the case. Usually, some other person, at some other time and place, often far away and long afterwards, who knows absolutely nothing of your previous action, will nevertheless repay you grain for grain. Every unkind word, every time you cheat, every time you lie, every time you deceive, every time you evade responsibility.

THE LAW OF GIVING AND RECEIVING

The Law of Retribution is a cosmic law; impersonal and unchanging as The Law of Gravity. Neither law considers any person.

When you "give with getting" as your objective, you might as well keep it or throw it away.

"Freely you have received, freely give."

Matthew 10:8

Give with a free and willing spirit. There is no obligation and no dictation attached.

Are you crazy Rev. Della? I worked 60 hours last week. It was not freely given to me.

What about the breath, the stamina, the strength and intelligence that you used for those 60 hours? Who and what did you pay for that?

The attitude of just getting all of the time is The Law of Life in a congested state. The first Law of Life is giving and it is the first law of all creation.

It is more blessed to give than to receive. You know why? Because in 2 Corinthians 9:7, *"Every man according as he purposeth in his heart, so let him give; not grudgingly, or of necessity; for God loveth a cheerful giver."*

Giving always precedes and predetermines our reception. Whether you are giving your thought, word, service or deed, giving gives you prosperity; a spiritual basis for permanent prosperity.

Giving makes your prosperity an automatic process not a sporadic process. Giving is your act of faith that you can move on substance (God) and manifests it as rich supply.

Tithing is potent because firstly it is The Law but also because it does some very important things for you:

† Tithing makes you actual partners with God. God is our sponsor who covers every check we write through our proper giving or obedient giving.

† When you tithe, you touch the "Law of Giving & Receiving" in a definite, orderly, systematic way of giving.

† You receive as you give. No more sporadic giving and sporadic receiving, but an even and constant flow of funds.

† You become more self-reliant when your funds are on an even flow.

† You become more confident as you become more self-reliant.

† Confidence builds a positive mental attitude which attracts success.

Are you really prepared to receive? Our preparations show our active faith. Instead of moaning and waiting, we are preparing and working.

THE LAW OF GIVING AND RECEIVING

Preparing and working denotes expectation and:

†   It stimulates your interest.

†   It disperses your doubts and fears.

In 1 Kings, the 3rd chapter, you can read to the story of Elijah, the prophet. When three kings came to him, they asked him to pray for them, that they would be victorious in battle and they might have rain to supply their soldiers and animals.

Elijah told the kings to go back to their camps and prepare for the morrow; prepare to receive the water they asked for by digging ditches.

They prepared for the rain by digging ditches and ditches were filled.

Elijah, knowing The Law, instructed them to prepare and made the way easy for them to receive. The key to The Law is: We are continually drawing into life what we give and expect.

Whether we attract good or bad, it is governed by this same principle. You invite conditions because you put forth your thoughts of expectation.

Giving is a very touchy subject with some people. Giving is not always done in the right way and sometimes the results of wrong giving make us say, *"I never will give again. It only brought me pain."*

THE LAW OF GIVING AND RECEIVING

I am not just talking about financial giving but all giving. Think about this, how do you give? To whom do you give? How do you feel when you are giving? What do you expect from your gift?

Nature does not support a parasite or a loafer but she gives energy to the ones that are struggling forward. Learn from nature. Remember pearls before the swine and dogs. Do not give your substance to anyone who cannot appreciate it or improve with it.

Do you give just for the pleasure of giving? Is that a real thrill for you? The look on someone's face when you give them something in love? If only a kind word? Force your expectations to keep abreast with your desires.

A house divided cannot stand!

"The wisdom of the prudent is to understand His (God's) *way; but the folly of the fool is deceit."* Proverbs 14:8

The Lord loves a cheerful giver. The Law serves a free and willing giver. He, who gives much, receives much. The reason why some people receive so little is that they give out so little.

Remember it is not about what you give, it is about the thought behind what you give.

THE LAW OF GIVING AND RECEIVING

"Bring ye all the tithes into the storehouse, that there may be meat in mine house, and prove me now herewith, saith the Lord of hosts, if I will not open you the windows of heaven, and pour you out a blessing, that there shall not be room enough to receive it. And I will rebuke the devourer for your sakes, and he shall not destroy the fruits of your ground; neither shall your vine cast her fruit before the time in the field, saith the Lord of hosts. And all nations shall call you blessed: for ye shall be a delightsome land, saith the Lord of hosts."

Malachi 3:10-12

That is when your *giving* makes you ready to receive.

THE LAW OF GIVING AND RECEIVING

Speak this out loud for yourself:

**"I have more than enough so it is my
pleasure to give. I love to spare and share.**

**I practice The Law of my loving Father. I
know it is necessary to give and give freely if
I am to receive freely.
The Law of Receiving includes giving. I give
for the love of giving.**

**I can more than afford to be generous to
others for my Father is so generous to me.**

**I give and I open my heart to the potential
blessings of every situation and
circumstance.**

**I give freely in many ways and my receipts
come from expected and unexpected
places, from expected and unexpected
people.**

**I release the situations of my life into God's
care and I am blessed!**

I let go and let God."

THE LAW OF GIVING AND RECEIVING

A coin held tightly in my closed hand won't buy me anything. It's only when I release the coin that I can invest it or spend it. Sometimes, I may hold a challenging situation in my mind as if I were clutching it in my closed hand, refusing to release it. I realize that by not letting it go, I am not giving it a chance to be anything other than a challenge.

In prayer, however, I release the situation into God's care. I let go of any attachment to outcome or eventuality and I invest my trust in God.

As I let go and let God be active in my life, I open my heart to the potential blessings of every circumstance. As my prayer life builds, I become proficient at releasing to God the things better left to God, which in turn lets me focus on what is mine to do.

"Then He said to them, 'Give therefore to the emperor's things that are the emperor's and to God the things that are God's.'"

Matthew 22:21

THE LAW OF FORGIVENESS

Jesus often spoke of forgiveness. He knew how vital the Law of Forgiveness is to our lives.

"For if you forgive men for their trespasses, so will your heavenly Father forgive you yours. But if you forgive not men their trespasses, neither will your Father forgive yours."   Matthew 6:14-15

"Judge not, that you be not judged for with what judgment you judge, you will be judged; and with the measure you use, it be measured back to you."
                    Matthew 7:1-2

Jesus proved His belief that forgiveness was indeed great power.

"...Father forgive them for they know not what they do."
                    Luke 23:34

<u>Forgive</u>

1a: to give for, to give up resentment of, or claim to requital for, **b:** to cease to feel resentment against anyone on account of wrong committed, **c:** to give up resentment of or claim to requital for an offense or wrong, **d:** to grant relief from, **e:** to give truth for error.

THE LAW OF FORGIVENESS

Forgiveness is a complete wiping out of error-thoughts from your consciousness and a full deliverance from the inharmony that the error-thoughts have produced.

When we forgive, we repair. Forgiveness uproots things harbored in the subconscious mind or memory. Forgiveness completely destroys the weeds in your mental garden.

Diseases are due to bottled up and/or suppressed grief and anger, anxiety and hostility, mental disorders and guilt. All of these things feed tumors, cancerous growths, headaches, backaches, mean attitudes and the dictations of negativity. Forgiveness absolves and liberates us from these sinful effects.

Hear me now.

The only way to overcome an unpleasant or hurtful fact is to forsake it, forget it or forgive it and the idea that started it. It is a waste of time wrestling with the fact itself. The fact cannot be changed. It is in the past and there is nothing we can do about the past, but learn from it.

The lesson we learn is never to do it just that way again because that way doesn't work for you. Forgiveness is the only means, which will enable you to become in accord, (in harmony), with The Law.

When you conceive an idea that is wrong, destructive or evil, and dwell upon it, eventually it will become a fact in your life, your world, and your affairs.

When you hold onto it in your mind, that someone has wronged, mistreated or misused you (not that they haven't treated you unfairly), you cannot be free of the wrongdoing or the injustice, as long as you hold the thought in your consciousness.

Jesus was the victor as He hung on the cross because He was able to forgive. The forgiver is always greater than his or her adversaries!

Let's look at Jesus in the hours of His greatest distress. He showed His character. Pilot, the governors, the high priests, the Sadducees, and the Pharisee were all shattered by His character. They thought they had Him. They exercised power over His physical body momentarily; by trying and condemning Him; by sentencing Him; by beating Him; by dragging Him through the streets and crucifying Him. But as they were trying to take His life, He looked down from the cross and saw their smallness of mind and He shouted out, *"...Father forgive them for they know not what they do."*

He was the victor; the superior. Greater than His adversary because He was great enough to forgive the wrong, the injustice, brutality, disrespectful meanness they subjected him to. He gave understanding for their confused and irrational minds. He gave peace for chaos; love for their hatred and blessed them for killing Him. What did He do? He gave eternal life for death.

But He also knew He couldn't carry the hurt and wrong that they had shown Him, with Him in the tomb, or He would still be there now. He released it right there to be free in His mind to gain the victory over death.

You cannot do powerfully great works with that stuff on your mind...in your mind. I am created in the image-likeness of God and I am designed to do most magnificent things. That is what I am concerned with.

I am not responsible for what you do or what you say. I am responsible for what I do, say or think about what you do or say. It makes no difference what you think of me, but it matters to me, my life, my world and my affairs, the way I think about you.

I refuse to give you free rent in my mind because you did something that hurt me. I refuse to help sustain the hurt, by keeping it alive day after day, in my mind... thus in my life.

I want you to really think about what you're saying and say this aloud:

"Right now, I forgive because it is necessary to my peace of mind and health of my body.

THE LAW OF FORGIVENESS

I forgive the hurts in my conscious and in my subconscious mind.

I forgive it all so that my Father can forgive me all of my mistakes.

I forgive to show that I am earnestly seeking the Holy Spirit. I am living under God's grace.

I put away all bitterness, wrath, anger and evil speaking. I am tender-hearted, kind and forgiving of all.

I forgive, for I do not want to fail in my demonstrating of my manifesting. I must produce good fruit. And it is impossible to do so, if my tree is full of med flies and pesticides. Med flies and pesticides will spoil the taste of my fruit. They will cheapen the marketability of my fruit. And I will find my tree being chopped down and thrown into the fire because of all its uselessness."

Hear me real good now! The quality of forgiveness must be as limitless as faith, hope or love.

You need to clean up your mind. Certain ideas must be dissolved and cleared from your mind in order that other new ideas, with different characters, can replace them.

THE LAW OF FORGIVENESS

Search your mind. Be honest with yourself. Is your thought realm filled with:

† Resentment?

† Feelings of slight and abuse?

† Things that you are holding against someone?

† Are you harboring congested thoughts that should be forgiven?

Don't worry about, *"Who did this or that"* or *"Why did they do this or that?"* Bless them and release them for your own sake.

A sick mind that refuses to release and forgives becomes sicker. It is in your power to be healed today. It is in your power to be forgiven for all your faults and shortcomings. You can forgive all those that have harmed you. You can have a house cleaning to the glory of the Christ inside of you. And watch the peace and prosperity begin in your life. When you forgive, you set forth a natural law to operate in a natural, unrestricted way.

"For if you forgive men their trespasses, your heavenly Father will also forgive you. But if you forgive not men their trespasses, neither will your Father which is in heaven forgive your trespasses." Mark 11:26

Peter asked Jesus:

THE LAW OF FORGIVENESS

"Lord, how often shall my brother sin against me, and I forgive him? Till seven times? Jesus saith unto him, 'I say not unto thee, until seven times, but until seventy times seven. Matthew 18:21-22

You need to clean up your minds. Certain ideas must be dissolved and cleared from your mind in order that the other new God given idea can take root and produce the wondrousness God has in store for you.

Remember Joseph's understanding after his brothers had treated him cruelly, feeling and knowing the truth. Tell those who try to abuse you (I say, "try to abuse you" because they cannot if you don't let them):

"Fear not: for am I in the place of God? But as for you, ye thought evil against me, but God meant it unto good, to bring to pass, as it is this day, to save much people alive."

Genesis 50: 19-20

THE LAW OF FORGIVENESS

Save your life today. Affirm this aloud:

"There is nothing anyone can say or do that will make me forfeit the calm peace of my soul!

I refuse to hold a grudge or hold anything against anyone for their attempts to wound me.

I do not give anyone permission to cause me to forsake the forgiveness of my Father God by making me withhold forgiveness from them.

I will not judge for I do not desire to be judged. So, my measuring cup of judgment is filled with love, understanding and forgiveness.

And so it is... Amen."

THE LAW OF ABUNDANCE

"I am a miracle in the making, through abundance and that more abundantly." The forces that generate prosperity are mental and spiritual.

In order to conduct a mental and spiritual war on poverty, you must first open your mind to prosperity. Most people with financial problems have a psychological block about prosperity. Some people believe that poverty is a Christian virtue.

You can open your mind to prosperity by giving up the ridiculous ideas that you have about it. Charles Fillmore says, *"The Father's desire for us is unlimited good, not merely the means of a meager existence. We cannot be very happy if we are poor."*

Nobody needs to be poor. It is a sin (mistake) to be poor. Dr. Russell Conwell who acquired eight million and then twelve million dollars says, and I agree, *"I say, you ought to be rich. You have no right to be poor. To live and not be rich is a misfortune and it is doubly a misfortune because you could have been rich just as well as being poor."*

"All things are yours."   1 Corinthians 3:21

"Seek ye the kingdom of heaven and all these things will be added unto you."   Matthew 6:33

Realize it is spiritually right for you to be prosperous; not to just get some money. Prosperity includes peace of mind, harmony, health and financial plenty.

Catherine Ponder tells us that there are between three and four thousand promises in the Bible. Many of them literal prosperity promises. Some theologians claim there are nearer to eight thousand such promises.

Many of Jesus' miracles were prosperity miracles and many of His declarations were "prosperity" declarations. Examples:

"Beloved, I wish above all things that thou mayest prosper."   3 John 1:2

"Prove me now herewith, said the Lord of hosts, if I will not open you the windows of heaven and pour you out a blessing that there shall not be room enough to receive it."   Malachi 3:10

"The blessing of the Lord, it maketh rich, and He addeth no sorrow with it."   Proverbs 10:22

"God is able to make all grace abound toward you; that you, always having all- sufficiency in all things, may abound to every good work."   2 Corinthians 9:8

"The Lord shall open unto thee His good treasure, the heaven to give the rain unto thy land in His season, and to

bless all the work of thine hand; and thou shalt lend unto many nations and thou shalt not borrow."

Deuteronomy 28:12

With God, all things are possible. All things, whatsoever you pray and ask for, believe that you have received them and you shall have them. Emerson said, *"Man was born to be rich, or grow rich by the use of his faculties, by the union of thought with nature."*

The Law:

† As above, so below, as within, so without. Your outer world of form and experiences is a reflection of your inner world of thoughts.

† The greater your awareness of the presence of God within you, the more that presence fills your consciousness and feelings.

† The deeper your understanding of spirit as the source, substance and activity of your supply, the more permanently that truth will be etched in your consciousness.

† It is your spiritual consciousness, your knowledge of the presence of God within you as total and complete fulfillment that interprets itself as every form or experience in your world.

THE LAW OF ABUNDANCE

Just a few of God's promises:

"They shall prosper that love thee. Peace be within thy walls and prosperity within thy palaces."   Psalm 122:6-7

"Thou shalt remember the Lord thy God for it is He that giveth thee power to get wealth."   Deuteronomy 8:18

"Let them shout for joy and be glad, that favor my righteous cause: yea, let them say continuously let the Lord be magnified which has pleasure in the prosperity of His servant."   Psalm 35:27

"Therefore I say unto you, what things so ever you desire when you pray, believe that you have received them and you shall have them."   Mark 11:24

Emerson, *"Man was born to be rich, or grow rich by the use of his faculties, by the union of thought with nature."*

God is the giver and the gift; we are the receivers. God dwells in us and this means that the treasure house of infinite riches is within you and all around you.

Hear me good now. Money is an effect. When you concentrate on the effect, you are forgetting the cause. And when you forget the cause, the effect begins to diminish.

When you focus your attention on getting money, you are actually shutting off your supply.

*"Blessed is the man who walks not in the counsel of the ungodly, nor stands in the path of sinners (*continuous mistake makers*), not sits in the seat of the scornful; but his delight is in the law of the Lord. And in his delight is in the law of the Lord. And in his law he meditates day and night. He shall be like a tree planted by the rivers of the water that brings forth its fruit in its season, whose leaf also shall not wither; and whatever he does shall prosper."* Psalm 1:1-3

"A good man out of the good treasure of his heart brings forth good; and an evil man out of the treasures of his heart brings forth evil. For out of the abundance of his heart his mouth speaks." Luke 6:45

You must begin this very moment to cease believing that money is your substance, your supply, your support or your security.

The reason for your depression when the money is low is that you have been separated from God with your faith in your money.

Now it is gone and fear sets in because you don't know how to get back to your source. If you never leave your source you don't have to worry about getting it back.

You must accept your position as the chosen one of God to receive absolute good eternally. Remember this always no matter how it seems, which is appearance and Jesus told us not to judge by appearances.

1 Corinthians 2:9, *"But as it is written, eye hath not seen, nor ear heard, neither have entered into the heart of man, the things which God hath prepared for them that love Him."*

Do you love God? Then don't worry about a thing! Light the fire needed to propel you with power into taking charge of your life.

THE LAW OF ATTRACTION

Attract means to draw. The Law of Attraction works at the unconscious levels to draw your prosperity to you.

You are (I am) a magnetic field of mental influence. Know this: You attract to you from what you are subconsciously thinking and feeling more than from what you consciously say you want.

I may say consciously that I want something but if subconsciously, I don't believe I deserve it or I am not qualified to obtain it, or it is too good to be true or there is a trick in it somewhere, I can't necessarily attract to me what I say consciously that I want.

Why? Because I attract according to my dominant thoughts and feelings. Please know this. We attract to ourselves things to which we give a great deal of thought.

You cannot talk one game and play another. You cannot think one way and talk another or act another way.

Now is the time for learning to think like Jesus, Jesus Christ, and Christ Jesus. I want you to attract the financial sources you need personally.

We can do this together. We just have to listen and learn. Putting what we learn into practice. Love *is* our attracting power. Love is the strongest form of attraction.

THE LAW OF ATTRACTION

Just think about how something you love stays on your mind and continues to draw your attention to it. If you love it deep enough, it will present itself to you or draw you to it.

Hate is one of the strongest forms of attraction. The world you live in is the exact record of your thoughts. If you do not like your world, you do not like your thoughts. Change your thoughts, change your mind and your world will change.

A depressed, anxious, critical, resentful state of mind becomes a magnet for trouble. It is imperative that you keep your thoughts clean and positive and keep a receptive attitude.

Don't let fear and skepticism block your channels for the entry of your good. Stop picturing yourself as weak or misunderstood. Stop dramatizing yourself as a martyr. Because if you do, there will be suffering. For that is what a martyr's consciousness requires.

Refuse to take on the troubles of the world. Withdraw any negative thoughts and feelings on all levels of your life. "I do not play with trouble."

When seeming troubles appear, you have to know they are temporary. Don't try to explain them. Above all, don't dwell on them. Release them and let them go out of your life.

THE LAW OF ATTRACTION

Practice expecting the wondrous things of God. Work out your own master plan for success by listening to the Christ inside of you. Realize that you cannot force your good, but you can invite it by dwelling upon its possibilities.

Do not spend your time merely hoping and wishing that everything will work out, invite the greater good.

How? By giving your attention to your desired good and attracting it to you.

How do you enter the promised land? By realizing that my promised land is unlimited good which my rich, loving Father has for me. My promised land is what I need it to be. I attract to me:

† Increased health
† Peace of mind
† More harmonious relationships
† Financial security
† More love
† Deeper understanding of my inner world of mind and spirit

I know success-minded people who are prepared for great success.

I am prepared for the great and successful adventures that are now attracted to me.

THE LAW OF ATTRACTION

Say the following aloud with your power and conviction:

I accept that I know the truth about money.

I have a fundamental right to be rich.

I am here on this Earth to lead an abundant life and to be happy, radiant, and free.

I should therefore have all the money I need to lead a full, happy, and prosperous life.

Why should I be satisfied with just enough to go around when I can enjoy the riches of my subconscious mind?

I will not allow anyone to make me feel doubtful or ashamed of my desire to be rich, at its deepest level.

This is my desire for a fuller, happier, more wonderful life. It is a cosmic urge; it is not only good, it is very good.

When my blood is circulating freely in my body, I am healthy. When money is circulating freely in my life, I am economically healthy.

I will not forget that.

THE LAW OF INCREASE

Prosperity is our divine birthright. It is the conscious awareness of God as:

† The abundant

† Ever present resource

† Unfailing

† Readily providing for all who open themselves through faith

Our contract states: *"They that seek Jehovah shall not want for any good thing."*   Psalms 34:10

That is a God-guarantee!

Prosperity is based on the conscious awareness of the idea that God's abundance is the underlying source of all things. You need to know this because things come and go but the idea of abundance endures.

Jesus, our Wayshower, had no visible possessions, but He could supply thousands of people with food. How? Through praising and giving thanks to the invisible spirit of plenty.

The difference between spiritual prosperity and material prosperity is founded on understanding; the inexhaustible, omnipresent substance of Spirit (God) as a source of supply. The material belief is that the possession of things, constitutes prosperity and that we have to suffer and struggle in order to obtain them.

Yes, success requires work. Work with yourself, not stress, pain, struggle, and strain. Our orders, *"Seek you first the kingdom of heaven and all these things will be added unto you."* Prosperity is a God thing. Your results can only equal your investment… reaping what you sow *is* The Law of Compensation.

Let's now work seriously with "success through The Law of Increase."

You must get the right understanding of the laws and principles upon which success is based.

† You must apply the right methods of operating these principles until you reach your goal.

† Don't procrastinate.

† Find the best and easiest way for all concerned to do what has to be done.

† Learn to eliminate. The wastebasket is as important as a file cabinet.

† Have the courage to say "no" and mean it!

† Have the courage to face the truth!

† Do the right thing because it is the right thing!

† Listen. Listening leads to information and understanding.

† Understand information is power.

† If God is your partner, make your plans larger; aim high. Don't settle for less than the best.

Success: Is the favorable or prosperous termination of attempts or endeavors. Success is an idea you have faith in and plan to work toward owning. The Law: "Whatsoever you can conceive and believe, you shall receive and when you receive you succeed."

To experience success you must have the idea and you must first believe it inside of you. You must have the idea and believe in that idea to the extent that you know, no matter the opposing appearances.

The doubts of family and friends are stumbling blocks falling in your way, that you must use as stepping stones; shortage in the cash flow; plans that seemed right that seem now to be going wrong. No matter, whatever. You are willing, and gladly so, to follow your idea until it manifests.

Why do you do that? Because you know for sure it will manifest to the fullest…however long it takes! You have to be the one who believes this as truth because most times, you will be the only one who does believe this. And believing is receiving after conceiving.

We live on to spheres of success.

THE LAW OF INCREASE

The Outer:

- † Family
- † Achievements
- † Financial
- † Vocational
- † Fame
- † Possessions
- † Friends
- † Service to mankind

The Inner:

- † Peace of mind
- † Happiness
- † Love
- † Character
- † Ideals
- † Discipline
- † Faith
- † Courage
- † Health
- † Contentment

In order to succeed you must thoroughly understand: The person who wins is the person who thinks he or she can win.

Trials only come to make you strong or give you information or build courage and tenacity. Sometimes the greatest obstacle may be your surest road to success. Your thorough understanding must be:

THE LAW OF INCREASE

I know God is within me, God is around me, God is through me. I can overcome any appearance of obstacles and the obstacles themselves.

To achieve success you need to increase in all of the necessary ways your success requires. Bless your work constantly. Know where you want to go, don't just wish for it! Find out how to get where it is and how to obtain what you want when you get there. Form the habit of doing things. The failures are the people who just talk about it and never do anything.

When you need it, know where to find it. If it takes study, then study more. Make your own decisions. If you don't make the decisions, you give others permission to make your decision for you.

Praise God from whom all blessings flow. Praise your work. Praise your mind, body and being. You cannot fly high like an eagle if you run with turkeys.

"Blessed is the man that walks not in the counsel of the ungodly, nor stands in the way of sinners (people falling short of the mark of divine perfection)*, nor sits in the seat of the scornful, but His delight is the law of the Lord. And in His law meditates day and night. He shall be like a tree planted by the rivers of water that brings forth his fruit in his season. His leaf shall not wither and whatsoever he does shall prosper."*

Psalm 1:1-3

THE LAW OF INCREASE

Speak the words of truth and praise God for His many promises. *"So shall my word be that goes forth out of my mouth: It shall not return to me void, but it shall accomplish that which I please and it shall prosper in the thing whereto I sent it!"*

When you speak of your project, do not speak of its challenges because there is power in your spoken word. You do not want to give power to your challenges. Speak the words for what you want to accomplish: the words you need to prosper.

Both Matthew and John recorded for us the words that Jesus used to increase a few fishes and loaves of bread to feed 5,000. You know the story. Jesus blessed what He had, then what He had increased and multiplied. The key word in the blessing is "thanks." Matthew says, *"He took the loaves and the fish and gave thanks."* John says, *"...and He took the loaves and when He had given thanks..."*

To raise Lazarus, Jesus lifted his eyes and said, *"Father I thank You that You have heard me. I know that You always hear me."*

Thanks: According to Webster, is an expression of gratitude, to God, in the form of a short prayer, before or after a meal. I give thanks for I know God is inside of me. God is all around me. God flows through me, to me.

THE LAW OF INCREASE

Refuse to allow your mind to be filled with past slights and hurts that hinder your clear thinking. You need clear thinking for it is what you need to fulfill and to manifest your increase. You can be forgiving, loving, tender-hearted, and kind.

Why? Because my success requires it. Forgiveness is what Jesus taught us to do so that we can have peace of mind and power of purpose in order to increase and succeed.

Hello out there...to whom it may concern. Hello inside me...nobody owes me anything. I don't owe anybody anything. I forgive you and I forgive me for letting you disturb me and now, right now, I am free.

These principles are equivalent to magic. These principles are like having Aladdin's Lamp. These principles' techniques bring forth an understanding which enables us to use The Law.

In using it, we stimulate our good and bring about pleasure, happiness and success. You cannot lose when this is the stuff you use.

THE LAW OF COMPENSATION

"And God said, 'Let the Earth bring forth the living creature after his kind, and the cattle after his kind, and creeping and the beast of the Earth after his kind: and it was so.' And God made the beast of the Earth after his kind, and cattle after their kind and everything that creeps upon the Earth after his kind: And God said that it was good."
Genesis 1:24-25

God said it was good that things reproduced themselves after their own kind. So, if I plant the seeds of strawberries, I can rest assured my crop will be a strawberry crop because seeds produce after their own kind according to the will and design of God. So, Paul was right on the money when he wrote to the Galatians:

"Be not deceived (Don't let anyone fool you) *God is not mocked for whatsoever a man soweth, that shall he also reap. For he that soweth to the flesh shall of the flesh reap corruption, but he that soweth to the spirit shall of the spirit reap life everlasting. Let us not be weary in well doing for in due season we shall reap, if we faint not. As we have therefore opportunity let us do good unto all men, especially unto them who are of the household of faith."*

Galatians 6:7-10

So,

> † We are going to reap what we sow.

> † If we want to reap, we must sow.

> † Don't let anyone fool you baby. That's the way it goes.

What seed? What do you mean? A seed is a generative center through which intelligence manipulates substance and produces *form*. Every thought is a seed and brings forth after its kind. The seed is the essential element of transmitting life.

Your thoughts are your seeds.

Every carnal thought or thoughts of selfishness, hate, destruction, jealousy, fear, envy, discord, in any form is a seed sown to the flesh. When you sow seeds to the flesh, you have to reap what the flesh has to offer and bear what the flesh puts upon you.

It brings forth mistakes and builds up flesh consciousness. The fruit of this sowing is death and corruption. Every spiritual seed is a seed sown to the spirit. Spiritual thoughts feed and nourish and build up the spiritual you, the real you; spiritual thoughts reproduce after their own kind.

The results are life and immortality to the whole you... spirit, soul, body!

THE LAW OF COMPENSATION

Where do we sow? We have several scriptures to guide us as where to sow. It is not only important that you sow your seeds. It is of the utmost importance where you sow your seeds.

"Give not that which is holy unto the dogs, neither cast your pearls before the swine, lest they trample them under their feet, and turn again and rend you."   Matthew 7:6

So get away from the dogs and the pigs, don't sow there. You should stay away from the dogs and the pigs all of the time but especially when you are sowing your seeds to strengthen your spirituality. Jesus explains the reason in His parable of the sower.

"Some of you, hear the word, you rejoice at hearing it, but it is not planted deep in your mind and your heart and your soul so it has no roots. Some of you receive the word covered with thorns but because you have been wounded so deeply by the cares of world and the deceitfulness of riches, by that I mean thinking that having them will make everything all right and when you get them you find that's not it. With your disbelief fathered by past experiences, you choke the word and become unfruitful. But when you receive the word into good ground you hear the word of the Lord and understand it: which also bears fruit and brings forth, some a hundredfold, some sixty, some thirty."   Matthew 13:19-23

It is The Law — you must be compensated. Formulating and holding a belief is planting a seed either way for good or for bad. It is creative thought power. Our minds are creative-thought in action.

Have you ever heard the expression, "Train of thought?" A train is a vehicle that delivers something to a certain destination. Train of thought is a vehicle that delivers its creative power into manifestation. When you send/direct your creative power to lack in any form, you create a poverty station. Then, you fill it with fearful, unhappy, sordid beliefs. Then, you bow down to them and serve them and all that they produce after their own kind.

What are you talking about Rev. Della? You tell yourself you can't handle whatever the situation is. This is a lie. Then you give yourself reasons to make this lie correct. And you sit in a rut and bow down to the lie and serve it. By doing this, all other thought is paralyzed.

You don't find what to do because you are reproducing paralyzed thoughts. Have you ever been asked for advice and you give it with good, caring faith? You give truthful information and the person listens until you've finished and then says, "I know, but you just don't understand." And they start back at the beginning again? They are paralyzed and cannot move out of the paralysis.

The word of God and the use of the word of God can release you to propel you to freedom and to higher heights and deeper depths. It is important to sow your seeds; that is if you expect to reap anything.

THE LAW OF COMPENSATION

Some of you want to harvest but you don't want to weed, plant, or take care of the garden. You just want to harvest. But Jesus is telling us where we sow is just as, if not more, important.

You will need to do some weeding also. You need to weed out all inferior thoughts by digging them out by the roots with superior thoughts. Replace ugly thoughts with beautiful thoughts; distressing thoughts with pleasant thoughts.

Learn to think constructively of all persons, things, all events and circumstances. Name it all good. Why? Because all things work together for the good of those who love the Lord; and whatever you name it, that is what will reproduce after its own kind.

When you think better thoughts, you will transform your whole existence for the better. As you train yourself to mentally look for the good, you will move toward the good and it will reproduce itself as the good you desire.

Form larger conceptions of the good and the good will become larger and find expression in your words, your behavior and your talents. Your life will improve and your fruits will multiply in all directions; some of which you were not even aware of.

Don't plant your seeds in "Times are hard." That will tighten your purse strings so tight even God will not be able to slip anything in it. Don't sow your seed in "Nobody cares about me and nobody loves me." It will produce after its own kind.

If you want to produce love, keep on giving love even though you don't get it returned right away. If you give true love, it must reproduce after its own kind. If you don't cast your pearls before the pigs and the swine, that is.

Don't plant condemnation. Plant praise because whatever you plant is what it will produce. Don't expect your crop to come up over night! But compensation means equal returns for that which is given; it means a balance of that quality or service that is extended.

Tend your own garden. Don't compete with anyone or anything. You violate The Law when you expect something for nothing. Always be willing to pay your way. If it is money you need, you plant money by spending money; without begrudging spending it. Release your money cheerfully.

I know to some of you this sounds crazy but listen to me good now. Of times when your money gets to a low level, you begin to tighten up and hold back. When you do that, you close the channels and limit the supply from pouring into you.

THE LAW OF COMPENSATION

I invite you to rise to a higher level of sowing and reaping. I invite you to have what you want by planting what you want so that it can reproduce for you after its own kind.

It will reproduce after its own kind, for it is the law of God and The Law is infinite. And through our expressing it in our lives, all things are possible to us and for us.

THE LAW OF SUPPLY

Have you noticed that we are never satisfied? I mean not for long anyway! God did not intend that we should be forever satisfied!

When one good is realized, another desire for a greater good develops. And when a higher state is reached, another and greater state will unfold and urge you on.

We live an advancing life. At least God intended us to live an advancing life. It is o.k.... no, more than that... it is right for us to seek to gratify all of our pure desires and ambitions. Daily, we should be drawing into our lives the things we most desire and we should expect to receive them. The principle is the same if we draw good things or bad things into our lives.

I've brought this to your attention before and here it is again. Seeing is not believing. Believing is seeing! The Law is founded on our beliefs, what our beliefs determine, and what we see.

All the supply that ever was, still is, and always will be. There can never be a shortage of supply because there will never be a shortage of God; and God is supply. Supply, God, responds to demand. Where there is no demand, there will be no supply. Where there is no belief that there is always God, always supply... there will be no demand and there will be no supply. You will always be poor as long as your demands of life are meager and you believe in struggle, toil, hardships and limitations.

It is not your vocation that determines your riches. It is your demand that determines your riches. I tell you all the time that I require a large supply of everything. I demand a large supply. When you think more abundantly, you will believe more abundantly and you will receive more abundantly.

The way you think is the way you believe and the way you believe is who you are and how you manifest. There's a saying, "I think. I believe. I am." I hope you use this.

Your mind is a magnet and as a magnet it draws what you point it at. Be it good, bad or indifferent. Our mental magnet is greatly reduced by worries and fears and we may even repel our good by weakening it with worry amid fear and anxiety.

When you allow your thoughts for good to become adulterated with thoughts of lack, you weaken your mental magnet. Because abundance and supply are one in the same...God! You have to think supply, talk supply and live supply. You have to keep your thoughts filled with ideas of plenty especially when things tend to look otherwise.

You cannot believe more in what you see than in what you're trying to think. That is why Jesus told us not to judge by appearances, but to judge the righteous judgment - which is right thinking followed by right action.

We tend to personalize supply and so we cut off the abundance of supply that is always available. What do I mean, "personalize"? We think that the rent, car note, phone bill and a few dollars in our pockets are supply. You force the other avenues of supply that are rightfully yours to close up. There is an abundance of supply everywhere, all of the time.

God is evenly present all over. So, supply is evenly present all over. If you think this and believe this, you can have this. Jesus demonstrated this in Matthew 17:24-27. Matthew is the only one to record this money miracle. *"...and when they were to come to Capernaum, they that received tribute money came to Peter and said, 'Doth not your master pay tribute?' Peter said 'Yes' and when He was come into the house Jesus prevented him saying what thinkest thou, Simon? Of whom do the kings of the Earth take custom or tribute of their own children, or of strangers?' Peter said unto Him 'Of strangers.' And then are the children free, not withstanding, lest we should offend them, go thou to the sea and cast a hook, and take up the fish that cometh first and when thou hast opened his mouth, thou shall find a piece of money: that, take and give unto them for me and thee."*

THE LAW OF SUPPLY

The collectors came to Peter. Peter represents faith. The collectors always come to our faith. Jesus didn't just get enough money for Himself; He got enough to pay for Peter (Faith) also.

Matthew was a most hated man. He was a tax collector and people hated the tax collectors then, more than you do now. Taxation could cause death as well as debtors prison. Matthew's social status would be that of a mafia member. He was called publican, sinner, traitor, and a swindler.

This is what he was, by his own admission until one day he heard Jesus say, "Follow Me" and he did. Matthew metaphysically is The Will, and we too must tell our will to follow Jesus, who is our spiritual awareness, or Wayshower, our Savior.

Matthew understood about money, he was a scholar. He spoke Aramaic, Greek and Latin. He was an expert in figures. Jesus chose Matthew so He had to have had need for Matthew's type of services because He certainly could have chosen anybody He wanted to.

Jesus realized that money is necessary for spiritual growth. Why? Because it frees us from material cares.

You cannot be thinking spiritually when you are thinking about how hungry you are.

Jesus' supply was unrestricted. He could draw it from anywhere. Jesus was so powerful He didn't even have to go Himself, He could send somebody. He sent Peter (Faith). He sent forth His faith when He needed money.

Peter's instructions were:
† Go to the sea.

† Cast a hook.

† Take the first fish that came up.

† Open its mouth.

† Take the money and pay the taxes, not only for Jesus but for all the disciples.

Jesus began by nonresistance. He dared to accept that His need could and would be met in miraculous ways. He used what was at hand and was fearless. He immediately said "yes" to the financial demand.

Jesus was in Capernaum when this occurred. Metaphysically, Capernaum means comfort and consolation. Capernaum is an inner conviction of the abiding compassion and restoring power of our being.

When we enter into a Capernaum state of consciousness, a healing virtue pours out onto our soul and transforms all discord to harmony. We must get into this state deliberately not because we are depressed or discouraged. It should be an everyday habit.

THE LAW OF SUPPLY

Jesus was in Capernaum when they found Him. He was already in that state of consciousness, so He didn't have to waste any time preparing Himself. Where there is a need to be met, know this, your faith is tested first.

Because there is prospering power in faith, there is always something you can do in faith in order to bring forth your unrestricted supply. With faith, you can take one step at a time and that is all you need to take... one step at a time... each step in faith.

- † Go to the sea: The sea symbolizes the mind of God; Universal Mind. That realm of unexpressed ideas that contain all potentialities for good. Going to the sea of God ideas is the way to begin successfully for the meeting of every need in life.

- † Cast a specific hook: Cast a definite prayer or prosperity decree into the sea of ideas and ask for divine intelligence. Casting a hook is getting definite. It is list making. It is picturing your good by using your imagination. Work with yourself for divine intelligence. I say every time you can, but at least three times a week, by thinking about it and claiming it and feeling it as if it were already done.

- † Declare that divine intelligence is showing me the way.

- † Take the first fish. Fish are ideas of increase. Use what comes as promised.

† Do not worry about catching more than one fish. Work with the idea in this lesson, only one fish was caught but it was sufficient for the needs of Jesus and all those around Him.

† Open its mouth; give the idea a chance to quietly unfold itself unto you. Like a child, an idea needs a chance to grow and time to grow.

† Privately, keep company mentally with your idea and the idea will tell you its secrets. Withdraw, to a quiet place and listen for the still small voice.

† Ask the Father what is the truth about this idea, "Father, reveal the truth to me. Let there be light now!"

† Become harmonious with your thinking. Dwell in peace and love, forgiveness and prosperity thoughts. Stop being envious, criticizing especially yourself, for former failures.

† Do not adulterate the process. Don't make it inferior by adding poor or improper substance such as doubt, negativity, fear, anger or impatience.

† Maintain purity of your thoughts, control your appetites. Know that you know what you know, and do what your Father will tell you.

Make these things firm in your mind and keep saying and thinking them until you believe it. I mean really believe it to be so true you can feel it all over, through, in and all around you.

These affirmations are a good start. Use them often. Take the parts that mean the most to you and remember them if it is only one line or one thought at a time.

The spirit of God inside of you will take you directly to what you need.

"I live and move and have my being in God. Therefore, I live and move and have my being in exhaustless wealth. God is my Father and all that He is, I am. God made me and I am one with Him and all of His wealth is mine."

Hear me real good now. It may be hard for you where you are on your level of understanding, but work with accepting this. All sense of lack is an illusion.

I know someone may be thinking, *"What is this woman talking about? My rent being due is no illusion!"*

You are right. The rent being due is not an illusion, but that there is not enough money for you to pay your rent is not only an illusion, it's a flat out lie.

You need illumination. You need to be awakened from your Earth sleep to see God as He is. He is abundance, prosperity, health, joy, peace and all that there is that you will ever need.

This is the difference between spiritual ignorance and spiritual understanding. God is...God is supply...God is manifest.

If God is, supply is. If God is manifest, your supply is manifest. But none of this will help you if you do not know it in the fiber of your being. *"You shall know the truth and the truth shall set you free."* You must expand your consciousness regardless of appearances.

When your consciousness expands to include the universal ability of all things invisible or visible, you will be able to understand and accept God is all there is. There is nothing else. This is my prayer always and I offer it to you: *"Less of me and more of Thee, Father. Much less of me and more of Thee."*

Let nothing or no one, even the fact that you have seeming poverty, dim your realization that your abundance is here, right now.

THE LAW OF SUPPLY

Say this aloud, really accepting it:

> *"My good is not coming in a while. It is,*
> *manifested right now!"* **Because God is**
> **manifest right now and all that the Father has**
> **is mine.**

> **As the prodigal son, all I have to do is arise**
> **(raise my consciousness), and return to my**
> **Father's house.**

THE LAW OF MENTAL ACCEPTANCE

"And when they were come to the multitude, there came to Him a certain man kneeling down to Him saying, 'Lord have mercy on my son for he is a lunatic, and sore vexed: for ofttimes he falleth into the fire, and oft into the water. I brought him to your disciples and they could not cure him.' Then Jesus answered and said, '0 faithless and perverse generation, how long shall I be with you? How long shall I suffer you: bring him hither.' And Jesus rebuked the devil, and he departed out of him and the child was cured from that very hour. Then came the disciple to Jesus apart, and said, 'Why could not we cast him out?' And Jesus said, 'Because of your unbelief for verily I say unto you, you have faith as a grain of mustard seed you shall say unto this mountain, remove hence to yonder place; and it shall remove; and nothing shall be impossible unto you." Matthew 17:14-20

Evidently, the disciples had the gifts because the man took his son to the disciples first. Evidently, Jesus had taught them the principles or the techniques or the whatever, because they were known to be able to do this.

They evidently thought they had it because they didn't understand why they couldn't do it.

THE LAW OF MENTAL ACCEPTANCE

"Therefore I say unto you what things soever ye desire when ye pray, believe that ye receive them, and ye shall have them.

And when ye stand praying, forgive! If you have ought against any; that your Father also which is in heaven may forgive you your trespasses. But, if ye do not forgive, neither will your Father which is in heaven forgive your trespasses."   Mark 11:24-26

So, it is necessary to:

†   Believe and

†   Forgive

"But without faith it is impossible to please Him(God): for he that cometh to God must believe that He is, and that He is a rewarder of them that diligently seek Him"

Hebrew 11:6,

What is the point you're making Rev. Della? My point is that giving is the first step to receiving. We must mentally accept that God is a rewarder. We must mentally accept that as a reality. The disciples had not really mentally accepted that they had the power necessary, and that Jesus had given them His authority to use them. They didn't really believe it, so they couldn't mentally accept it.

Psychologists say that you can have anything that you can mentally accept. But you must mentally accept it, first. If you cannot mentally accept it, you cannot get your desired good no matter what else you do.

You must learn that "the power of thought" is a means for attaining life's goals. You sometimes rush trying to bring about that which you are not mentally prepared to receive. Thought is power and power always performs as power.

You can get what you want temporarily but you cannot keep it because you have not first developed a mental acceptance of it. This was the purpose of writing the book "The Prosperity Commandments" and explaining how to use them. I wanted to prepare you to become mentally able to accept your promised land and to stay in it, enjoying the rich gifts of our loving Father.

Success in some cases may come gradually. Good, because gradual success is a more lasting success. Gradual success leads the subconscious to acceptance of your good degree by degree. Lasting success is a progressive process. It does not usually come as a flash flood of overnight wealth.

Sometimes, it does. Someone won three hundred and forty million dollars from a Lotto ticket. But that is rare and very far in between. It's a chance of a 147 million to one. Winning the lottery is an exception, as is winning at gambling. Nevertheless, if you do any of these things and you have not mentally accepted it, you cannot keep it, or use it effectively because of your lack of mental acceptance.

There must be an in-working before there can be a successful outworking; *"As within so without."* Let's look in Numbers, which denotes being in the wilderness.

In Chapter 13, Moses sends some young men into Eshcol to see if it was indeed the Promised Land; to look it over and see if they should go in there. To see what the people were like, the crops, the living conditions and so forth. They're sending a scouting party to Eshcol. By the way, Eshcol symbolizes "Great fruitfulness or abundant possibilities." They didn't know that or they would have just marched on in.

The first thing the scouts did was to cut down a cluster of grapes so large, that they had to carry it on a pole between two men. They stayed in Eshcol forty days. The number forty indicates a time of completion with something to follow. They were there and the trip was completed; they didn't know that! They returned and made their report.

They said it was a magnificent land, a land of milk and honey and they showed them the large clusters of grapes, figs and pomegranates. Then, ten of the scouts gave reason after reason as to why they should not go there.

Chapter 14 is about them scaring the people with their reports and the people acting crazy. Joshua and Caleb started tearing off their clothes in disgust and protest and told the people, *"It is a wonderful country and the Lord loves us. He will bring us to safety in this land and will give it to us. Do not rebel against the Lord, do not fear the people of the land for they are bread for us to eat. The Lord is with us and He has removed His protection from them. Do not be afraid of them."* Numbers 14:-79

Then ten scouts were not mentally prepared to accept abundance. Joshua and Caleb were. Caleb means bold and fearless. He was from the tribe of Judah, which symbolizes "increase and accumulation." Joshua was from the tribe of Ephraim, which means "doubly fruitful."

This is a pathetic example of people rejecting their good because they do not have the faith, which would give them the nerve to go up and possess it.

Have you ever noticed that the moment a negative minded person thinks he cannot get something done, he begins to knock it? There are times when people will belittle the very blessing that they are reaching out for. They may even belittle the thing they want the most. The thing they ought to have and most of the time could very easily have. They are not mentally acceptable to it.

Fear, doubt, failure, and complexities are things that keep you mentally unable to accept that you are good enough or deserving or whatever enough; demented reasons...you know what yours are.

THE LAW OF MENTAL ACCEPTANCE

Those who cannot mentally accept greater abundance, never experience it. That is why after taking the Prosperity Commandment Study, some people produce results while others don't!

In order to use the Prosperity Law of Mental Acceptance, we must:

† Release the past because the past is full of limitations and errors; the thoughts they make you think are destructive.

† Mentally accept the possibility and the probability of something better for yourself.

I know releasing past limitations can be very uncomfortable and difficult. We are creatures of habit and we get so attached to old patterns of living that we don't think we can get along without them. As long as you think that way, you are right... you cannot.

But know you are standing in your own way. For God can only do for you what He can do through you. Jesus always inquired of the sick, *"Do you want to be healed? Do you believe I can do this?"* You must give up the old thoughts and replace them with new, limitless thoughts. You must give up something for the prosperity you want. You must make a space for your prosperity. It may be the release of something tangible such as a no longer useful possession.

Or it may be something intangible such as self-pity, bitterness, or that belief that you have had a hard time and you will never let it happen again.

Thinking about it all of the time means you expect it to happen again and you get what you expect. So, it "will" happen again even stronger because you've fed it with the power of your thoughts and so now you have made it stronger.

Here we are back to reaping what you sow. Like begets like; things reproduce after their own kind. I am a magnet drawing to me the things that I believe, want, or need. Your good, which is God, does not reject you but you may have rejected your good by holding onto someone or something from the past.

How Rev. Della? Through resentment, hate, unforgiving, criticism, and emotional attachments. That, which you hold onto, keeps you in your wilderness. If you continue to hold onto negative beliefs about your past and present, you will bog down in your wilderness experiences indefinitely. You are the killer of your potential good this way.

Stop saying you've had a hard time in life. This keeps you attached to hard experiences emotionally and it feeds them and keeps them alive. As long as they live in your life there is not room enough in your thoughts and feelings for better experiences.

THE LAW OF MENTAL ACCEPTANCE

Let those thoughts go. Release them, forgive them and give up the past; until you reach the point where you take only the good (the God) from each experience. And let the rest go. Your progress into a happy life will be swift and certain but you must mentally accept this.

To mentally accept the good is simply to change your point of view. Change your mind and change your life. Romans 12:2, *"Be not conformed to this world: but be ye transformed by the renewing of your mind, that ye may prove what is that good, and acceptable, and perfect, will of God."* Mentally accept that another set of circumstances is possible, and then dwell upon that possibility constantly.

We have been teaching constantly that your thoughts have power. Use that knowledge. Put the power of your thoughts on the solutions that God will give you and stop feeding the problem. Use times of waiting as times of faith, which will give you patience.

And while you are waiting, use that time for preparation time. Expectation takes time. When you have done sufficient inner work, the outer results shall come or else God, Jesus, and the Holy Spirit have all lied. If you believe that, you are all the way stupid.

This is the definite way to reach our goals because, *"Without faith it is impossible to please Him: for he that cometh to God must believe that He is, and that He is a rewarder of them that diligently seek him."*

Repeat these affirmations as often as possible. Slowly, so you can feel them. Let the inner you tell you the one you need to work on most:

Because I believe that God is a rewarder of them that diligently seek Him, I seek Him.

I am using my Prosperity Commandments and I am mentally accepting my promised land.

I am in my promised land enjoying the rich gifts of my loving Father.

I affirm and mentally accept there is something better for my life, world, and affairs.

Vast improvements come quickly now in every phase of my life.

Every day, in every way, all things are getting better and better for me.

Feel that. Really feel that. Let's take that again.

"I take only the good from each experience. I let the rest go and my progress is swift, happy, and certain."

THE LAW OF MENTAL ACCEPTANCE

**"I bless my past for all of its lessons. I let it go
now to receive my blessings."**

I want you to know we are of the mind of Joshua and
Caleb, *"Let us go up at once and possess it for we are
well able to take it."*   *Numbers 13:30*

www.ingramcontent.com/pod-product-compliance
Lightning Source LLC
LaVergne TN
LVHW021539080426
835509LV00019B/2724